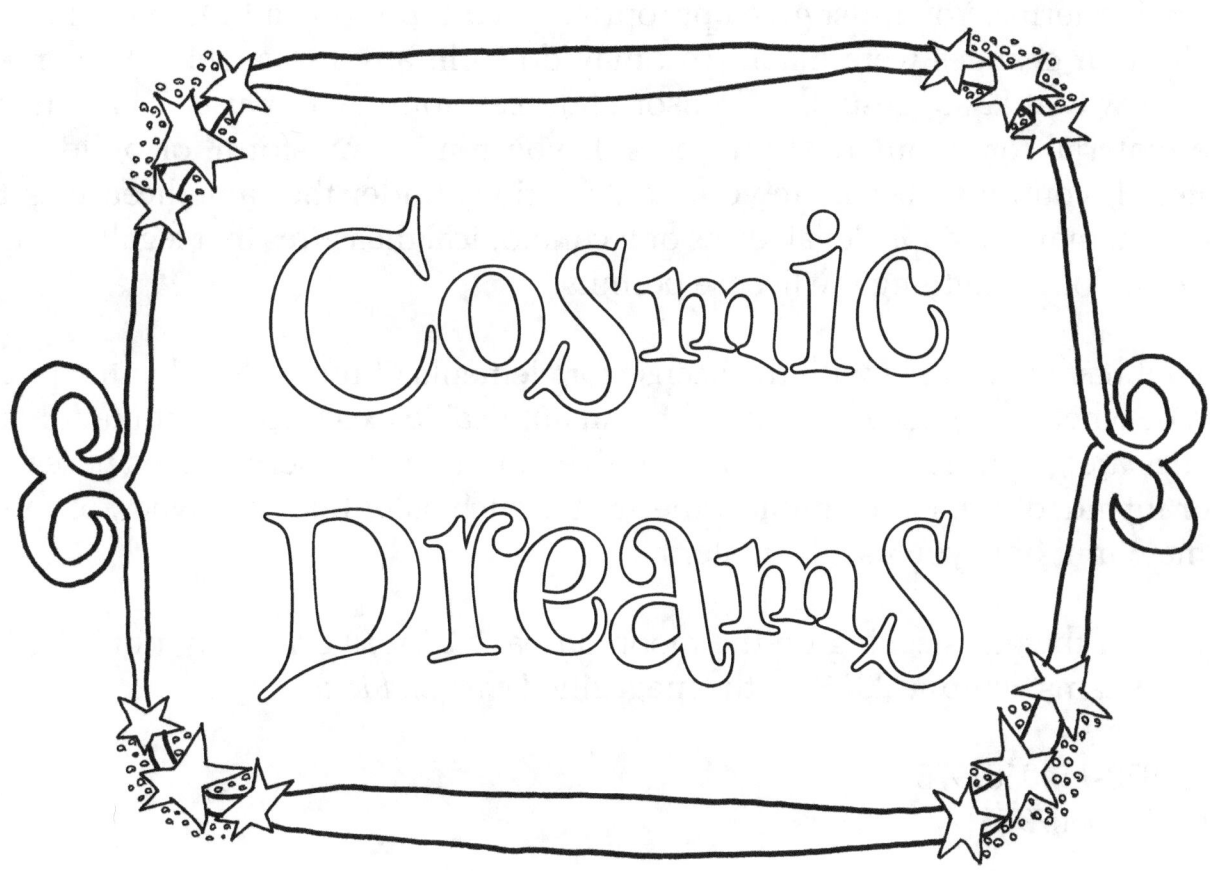

Cosmic Dreams by Timothy and Theodore Ashford
www.etsy.com/shop/childhoodtwopointoh
www.theodoreashford.com

The image of the girl sleeping on the moon on page 25 was originally published as "Cosmic Dreams" in June 2016 for the magazine *Letter and Line*.

ISBN-13: 978-1540607973
ISBN-10: 1540607976

First Edition

Interior designed by Timothy and Theodore Ashford
Cover design by Ashwords Design

Introduction

I am a superhero. And so are you.

The problem is that as we've grown up, we've forgotten this. In the hectic humdrum of our lives, we start thinking that we're average, ordinary, not capable of anything special. But we didn't always think like this.

As children, we knew better. We were astronauts. We were ballerinas. We could fly. We could run with cheetahs and swim with dolphins. We could even become dinosaurs.

So what happened?

At some point in our lives, some well-meaning person came along and told us we were wrong. Cheetahs can run about 60 miles per hour, after all, and yet the fastest humans rarely surpass 20 miles per hour. Of course we can't run with cheetahs. So we did what we were told to do, and we locked our inner child away in the deep, dark recesses of our mind.

It wasn't long before we realized this was a mistake, but by then we were too invested. Too afraid of being told that we were wrong again, so we ignored the cries of our inner child from their prison until we could no longer hear them. Many people are not even sure if their inner child exists anymore, and so live their lives in a constant state of gray.

I'm here to tell you that your inner child is not dead. You just have to be willing to let them come back out and play once in a while. Maybe you've forgotten how to play. I know I had for several years.

Then I remembered something. I used to be able to hop on stars and soar to destinations only I had ever seen. It didn't matter when my grandma had first informed me that stars were hot to the touch. I still knew I could land on one, and I planned to do so someday.

What you hold in your hands is the realization of my dream. Maybe the stars in our universe are too hot to touch as my grandma had said, but the stars in the world of imagination can be anything you want them to be.

So grab your favorite tools and start coloring in any way you please. I've even used crayons and have loved the results. Let your inner child speak. Color outside the lines. Try coloring in bright neon colors or in different shades of your favorite color. Try mixing materials. Try using impromptu materials if you're feeling daring, such as a piece of candle wax in place of a crayon. Or you could rub a brightly colored flower on the page. Or why not try potato stamps? What art adventures did you do as a child?

Let the drawings in this book inspire you and help you access your inner child. They have a range of difficulties, depending on what kind of challenge you're in the mood for. Most of the drawings feature a fair amount of stardust as well, which could either be considered easy or challenging to color, depending on how you approach it. My husband likes to color the background first and then dot each speck of stardust with a metallic marker, and I love the effect this gives. Other people have different ways of handling them. Some people don't even color the stardust at all, preferring to leave it blank. All of these are valid ways of coloring.

So just let your imagination run loose, and don't worry about doing things "right". My trying to insist on doing things "right" nearly caused this book to not be published. Several times. But my inner child won out. Even in this book, my art has mistakes. But I had to remind myself, just as I'm reminding you, that perfection isn't the point of this book. This book is all about tapping into one's inner child, and all children once knew that there was nothing wrong with drawing a head shaped like a potato. What was important was that they drew it. And colored it.

So here is my gift to you. It's not perfect, but nothing from one's inner child is. Take it and make a mess of it. Your inner child will thank you.

Timothy Ashford

One Night,

a girl had a

Dream...

Cosmic Dreams

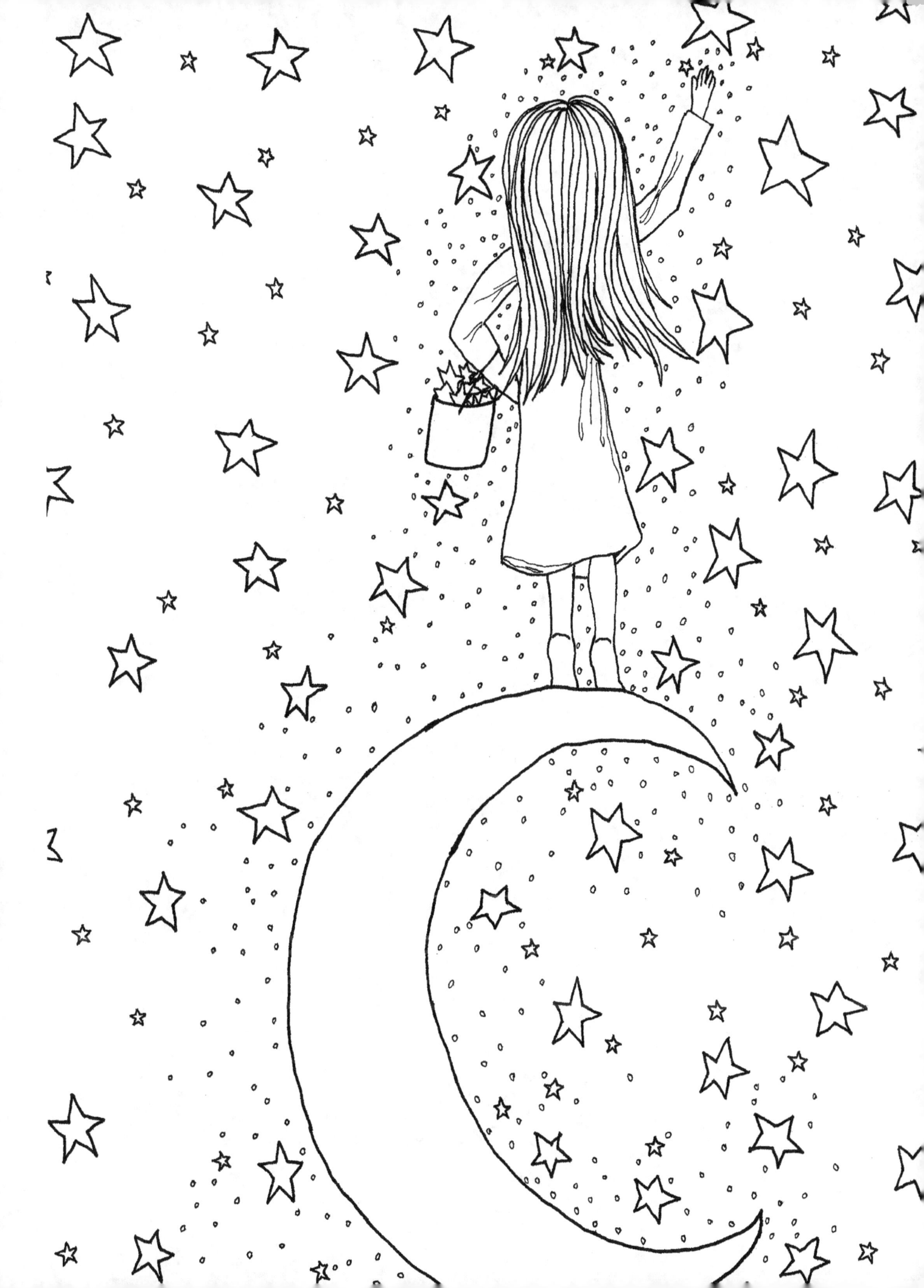

☆⭐☆ ⭐☆ ☆⭐☆ Cosmic Dreams

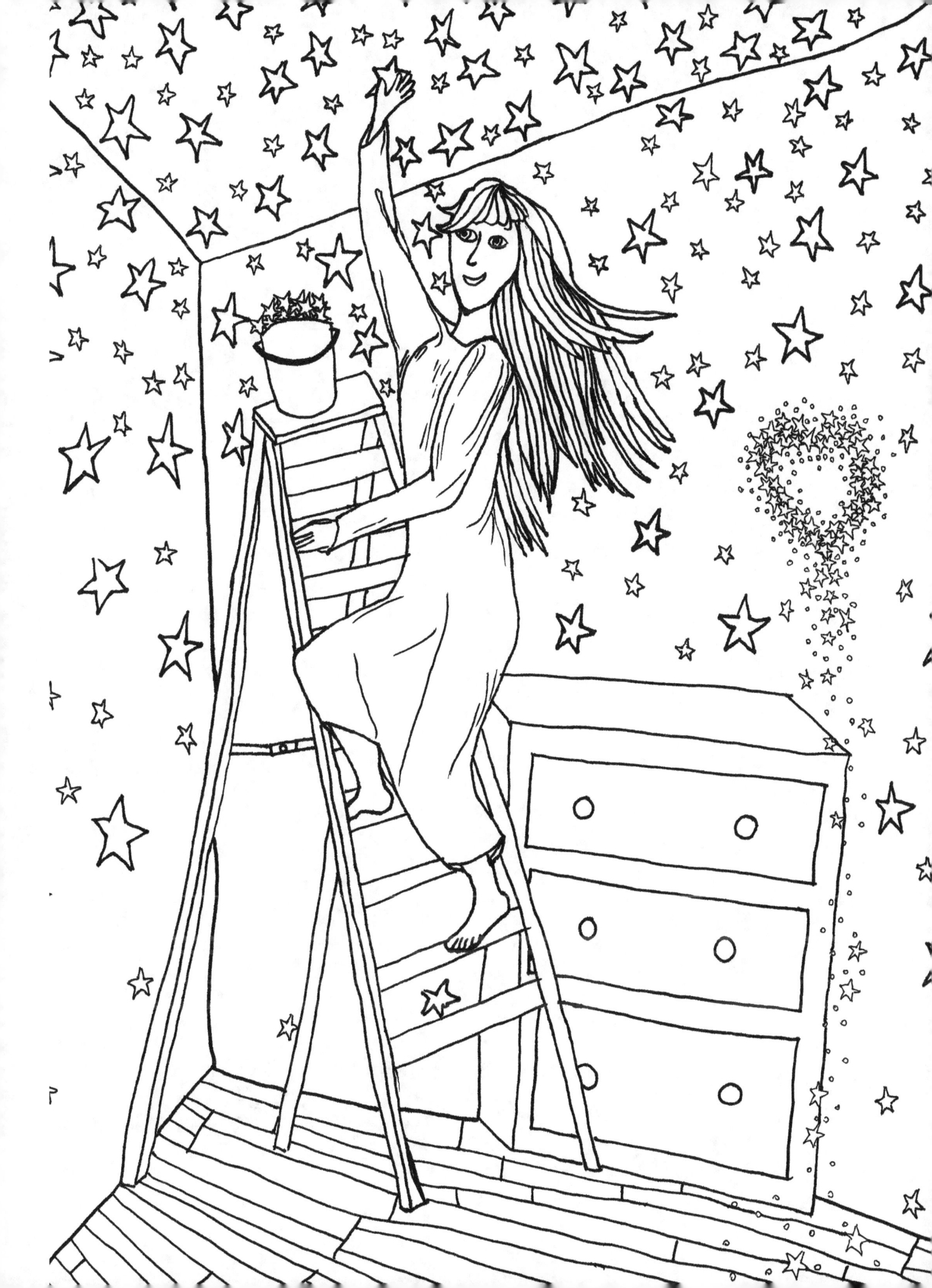

Cosmic Dreams

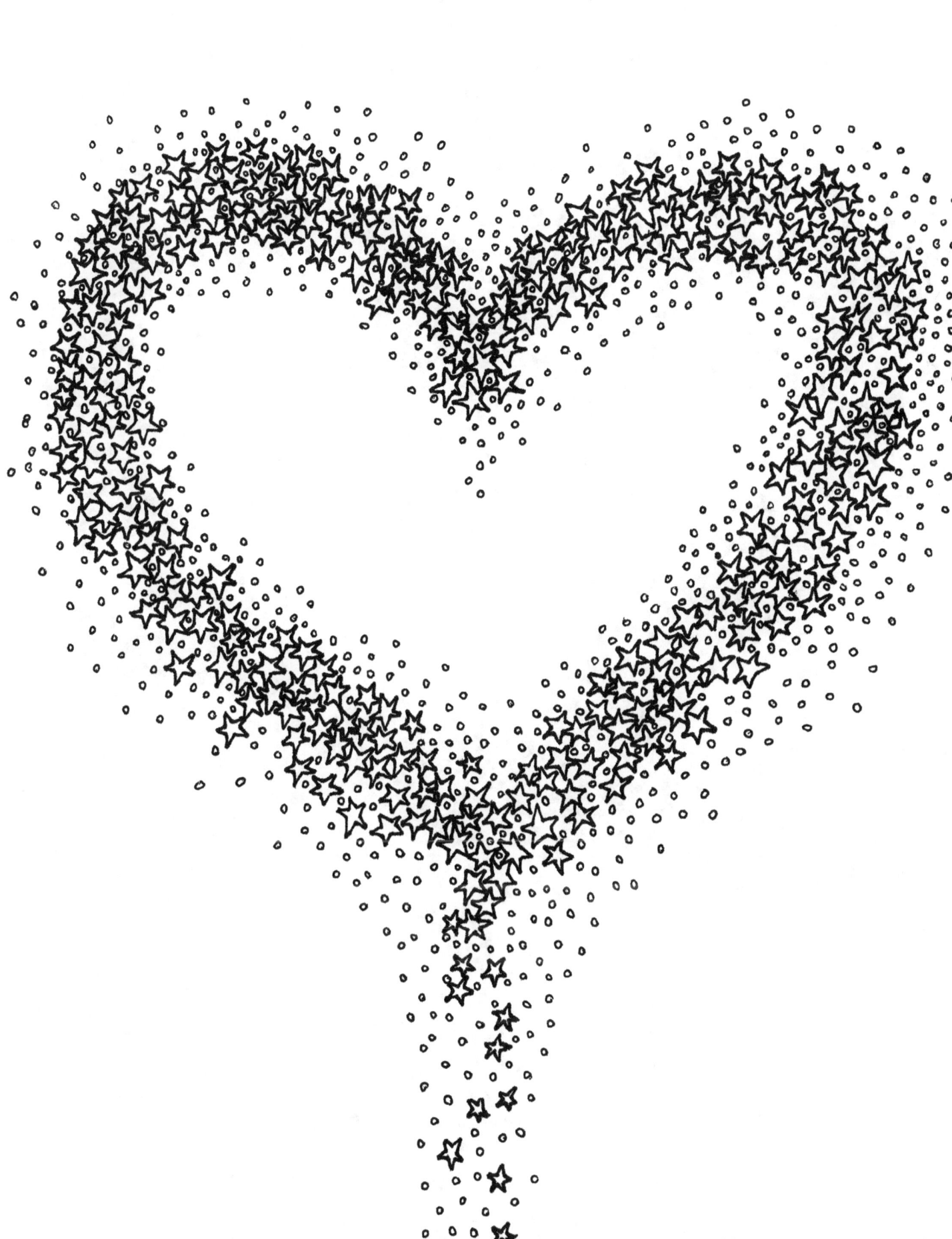

Cosmic Dreams

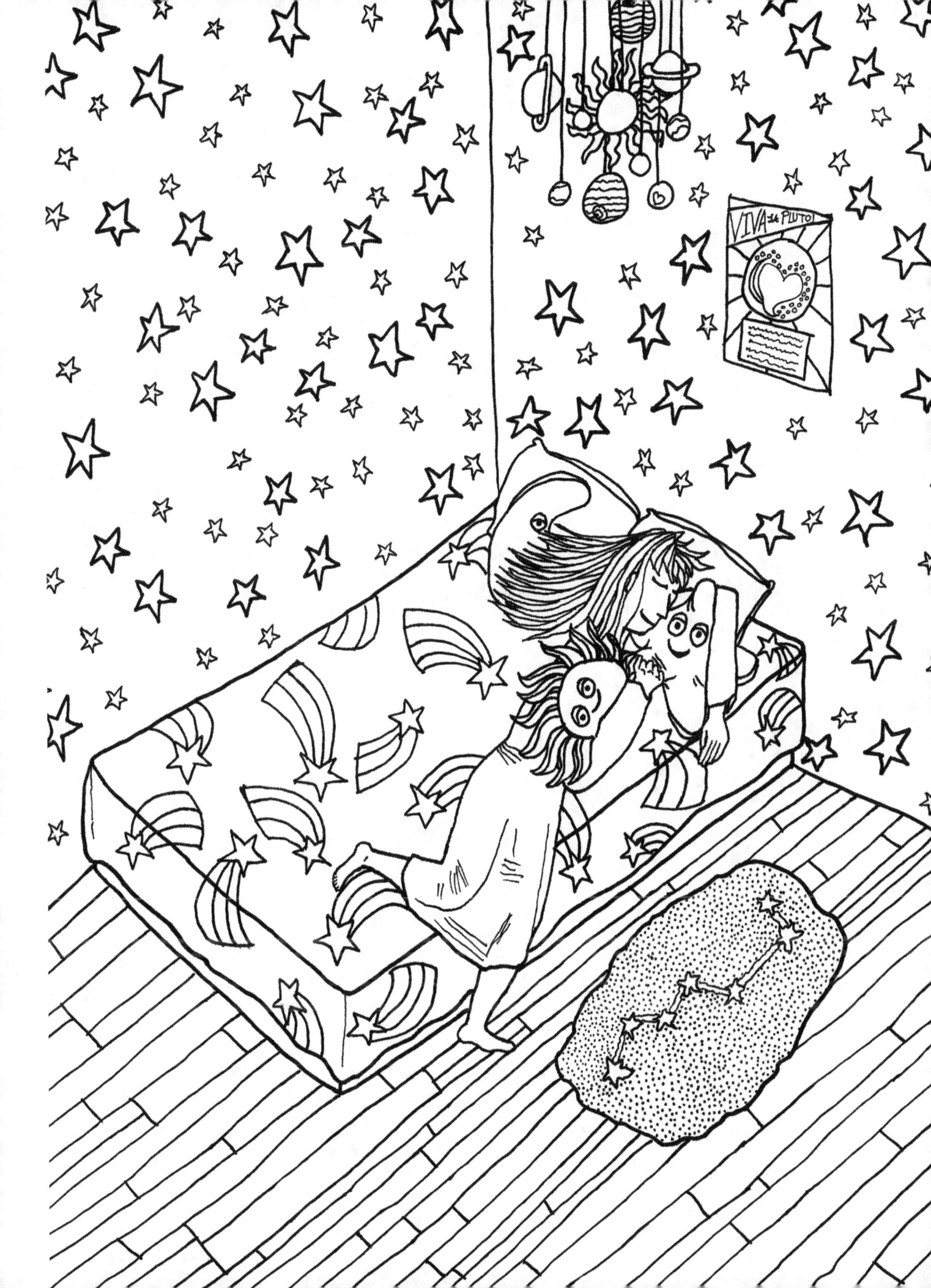

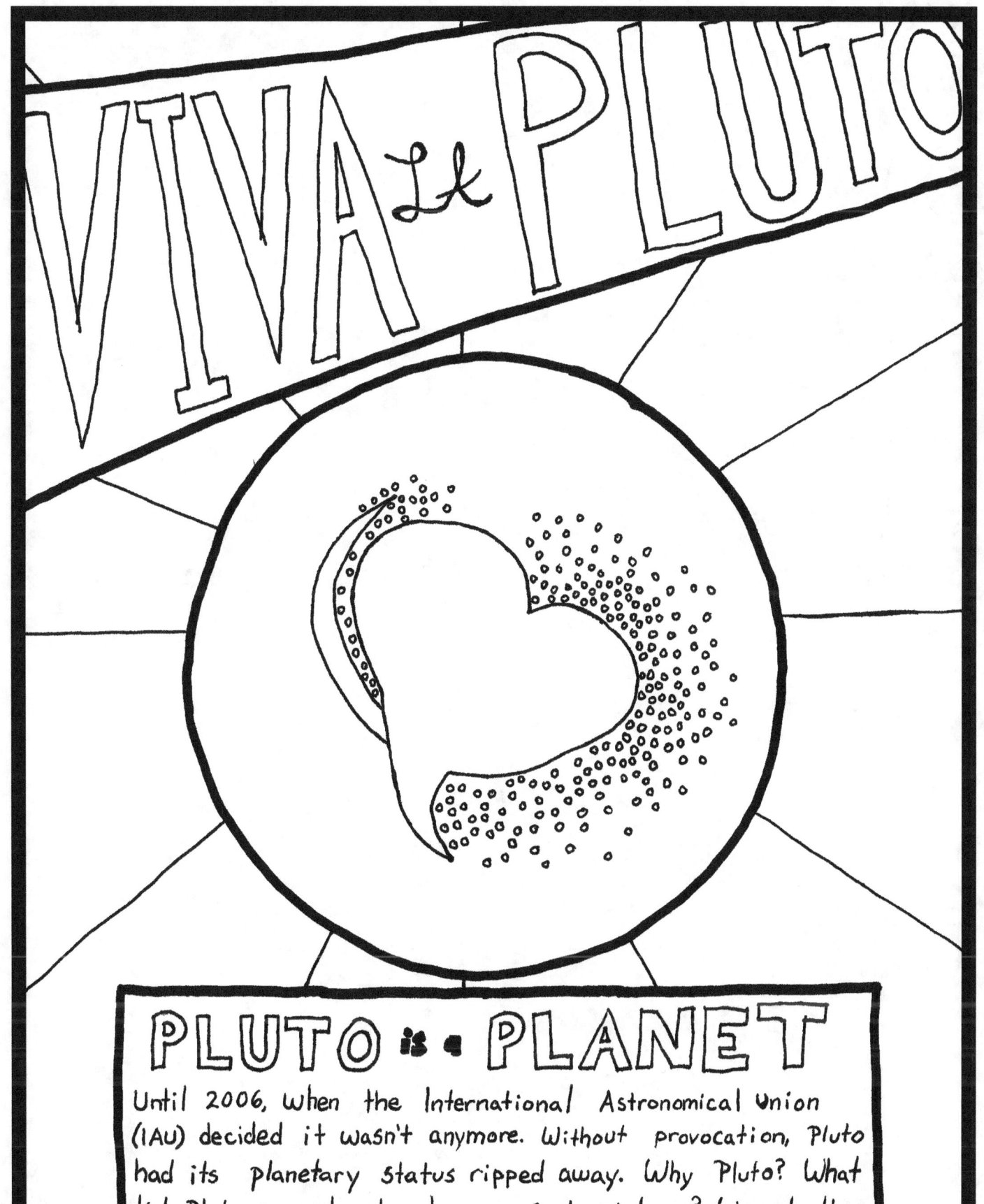

Cosmic Dreams

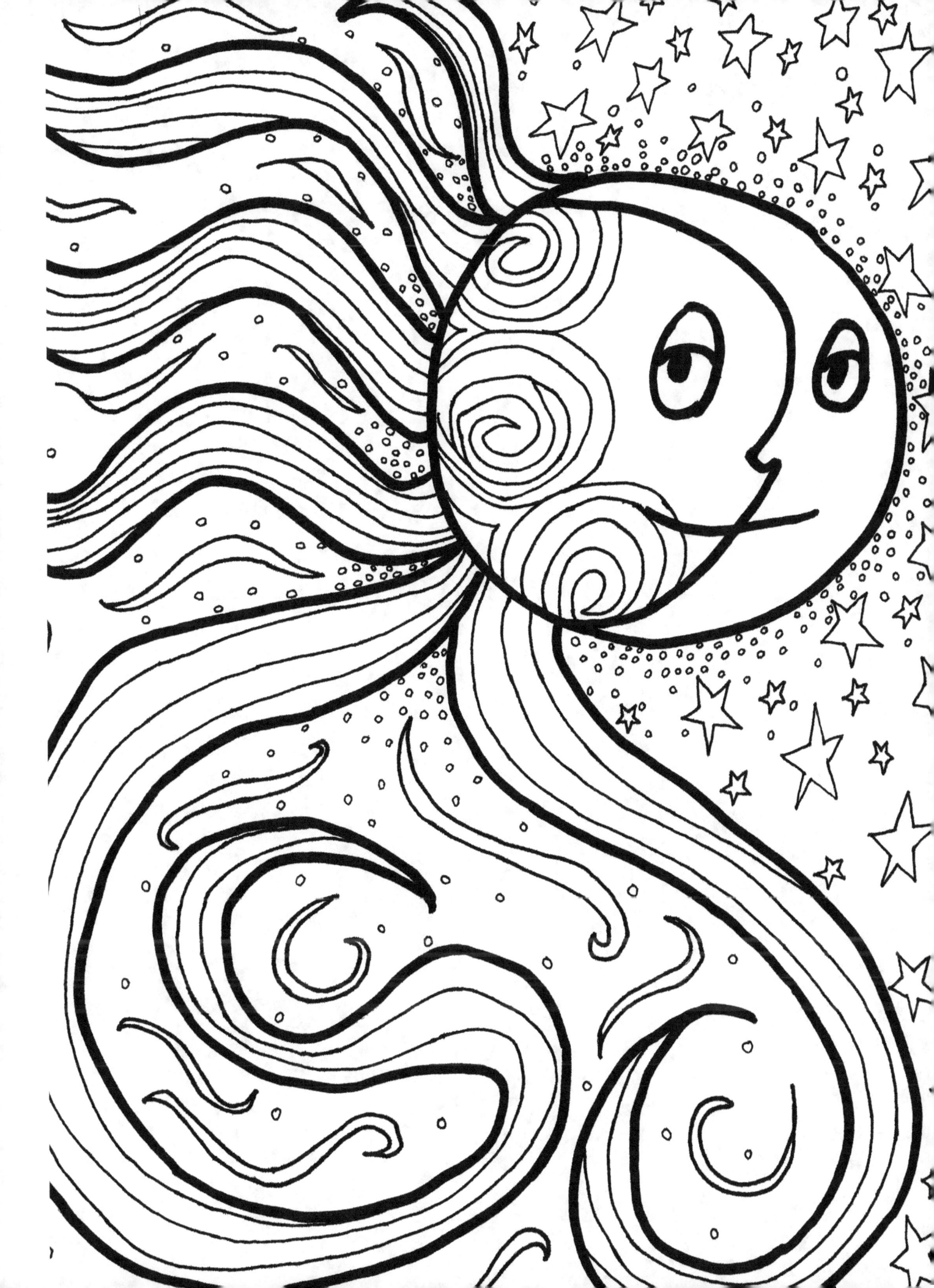

Cosmic Dreams

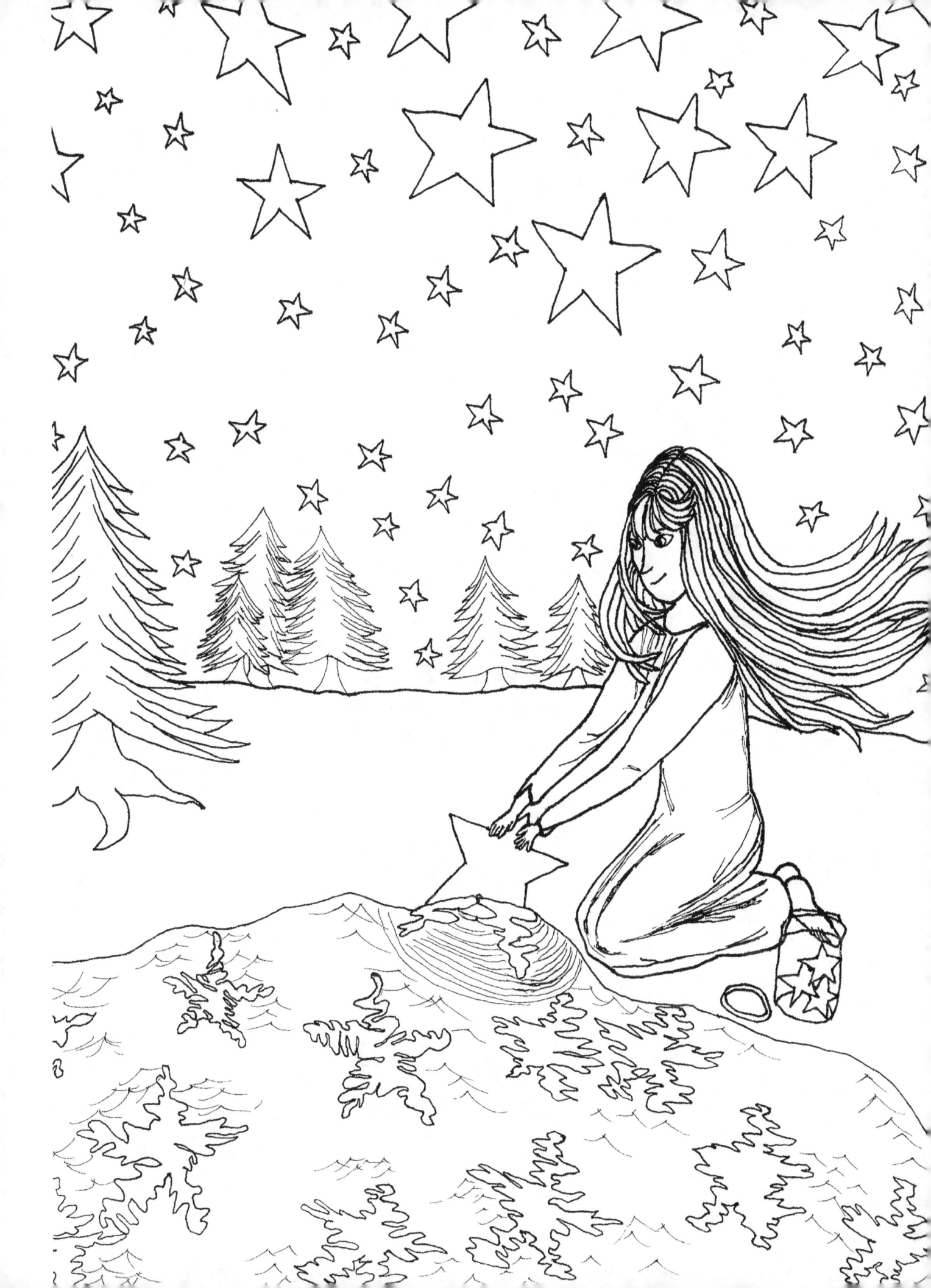

Cosmic Dreams

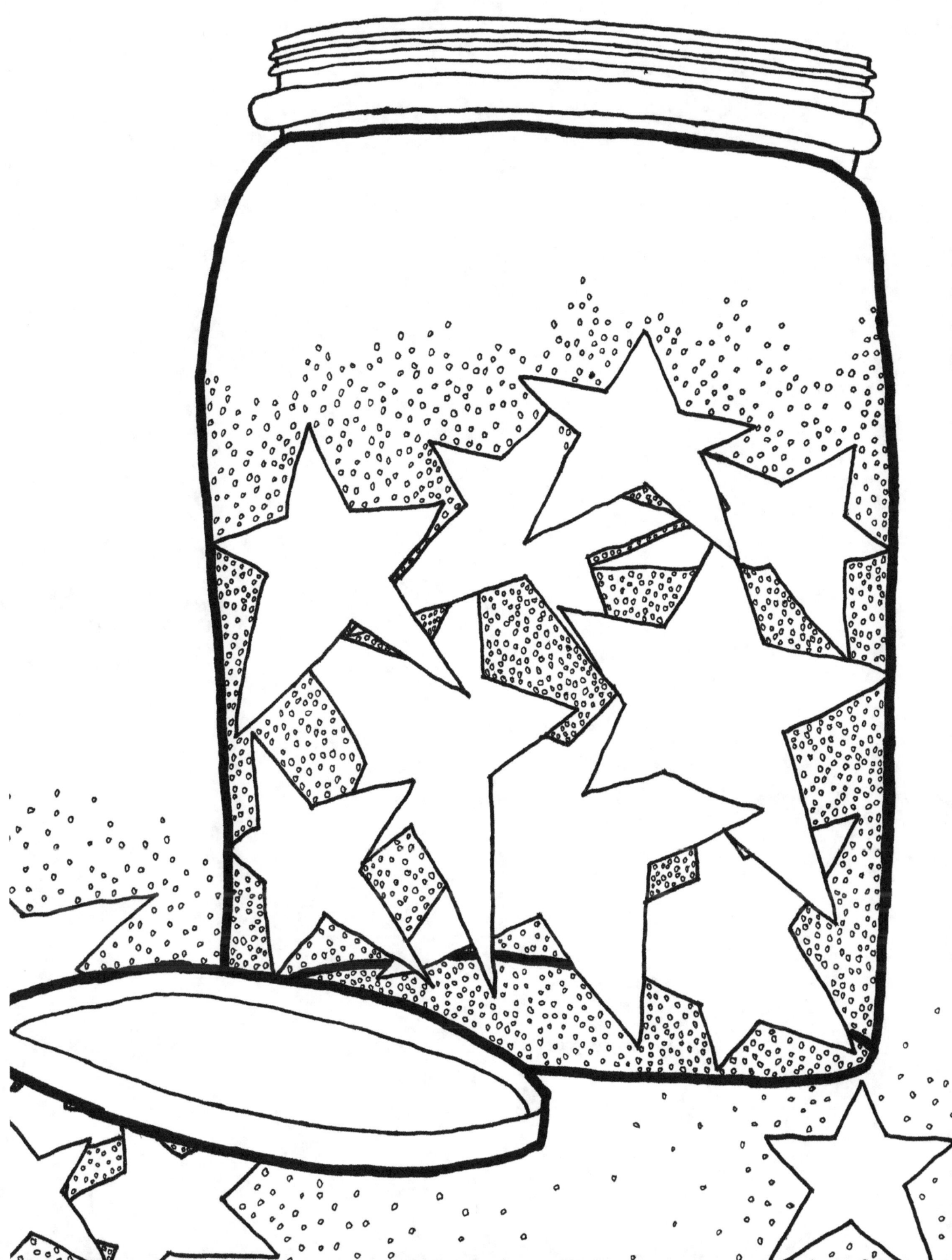

Cosmic Dreams

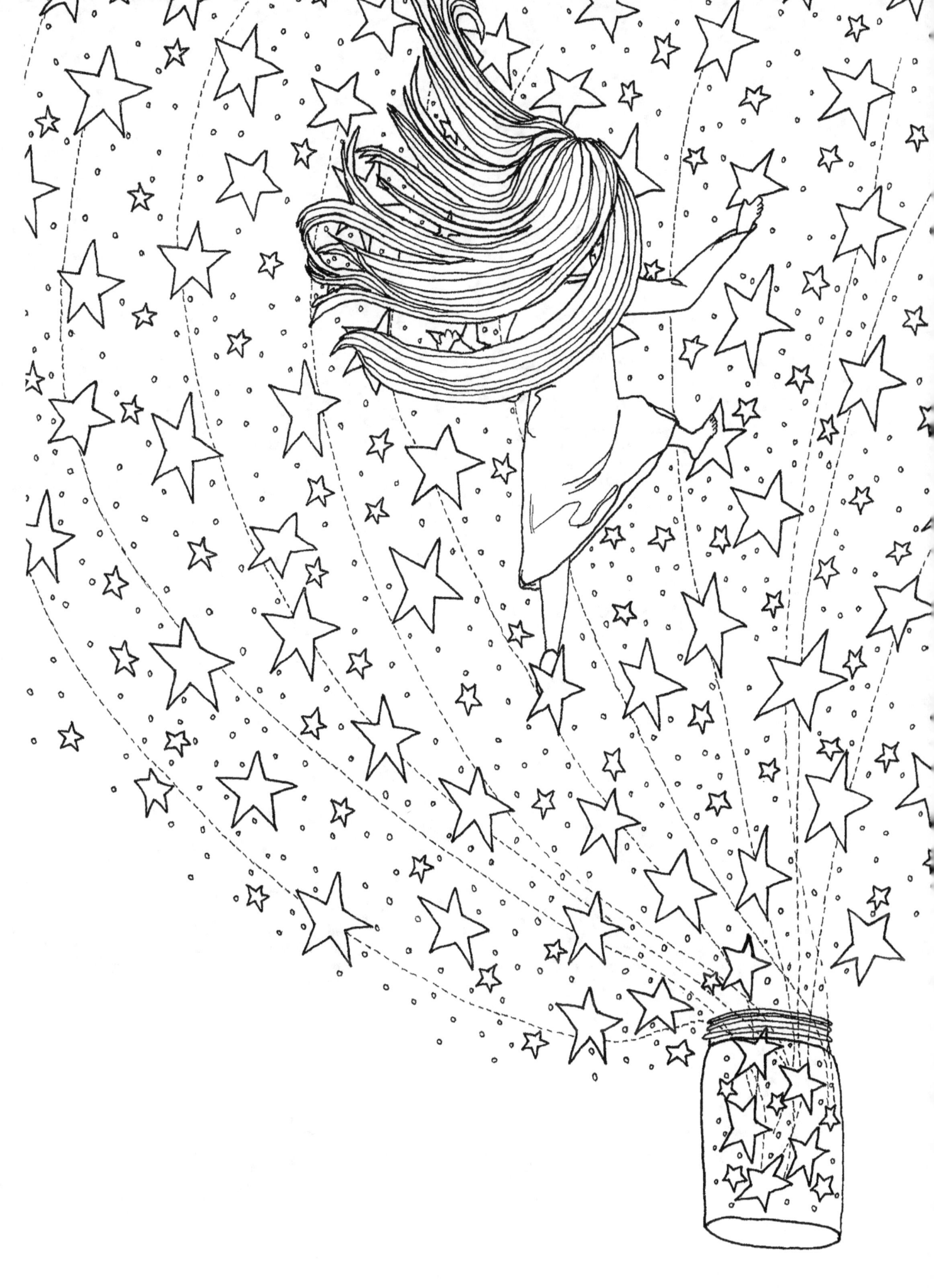

Cosmic Dreams

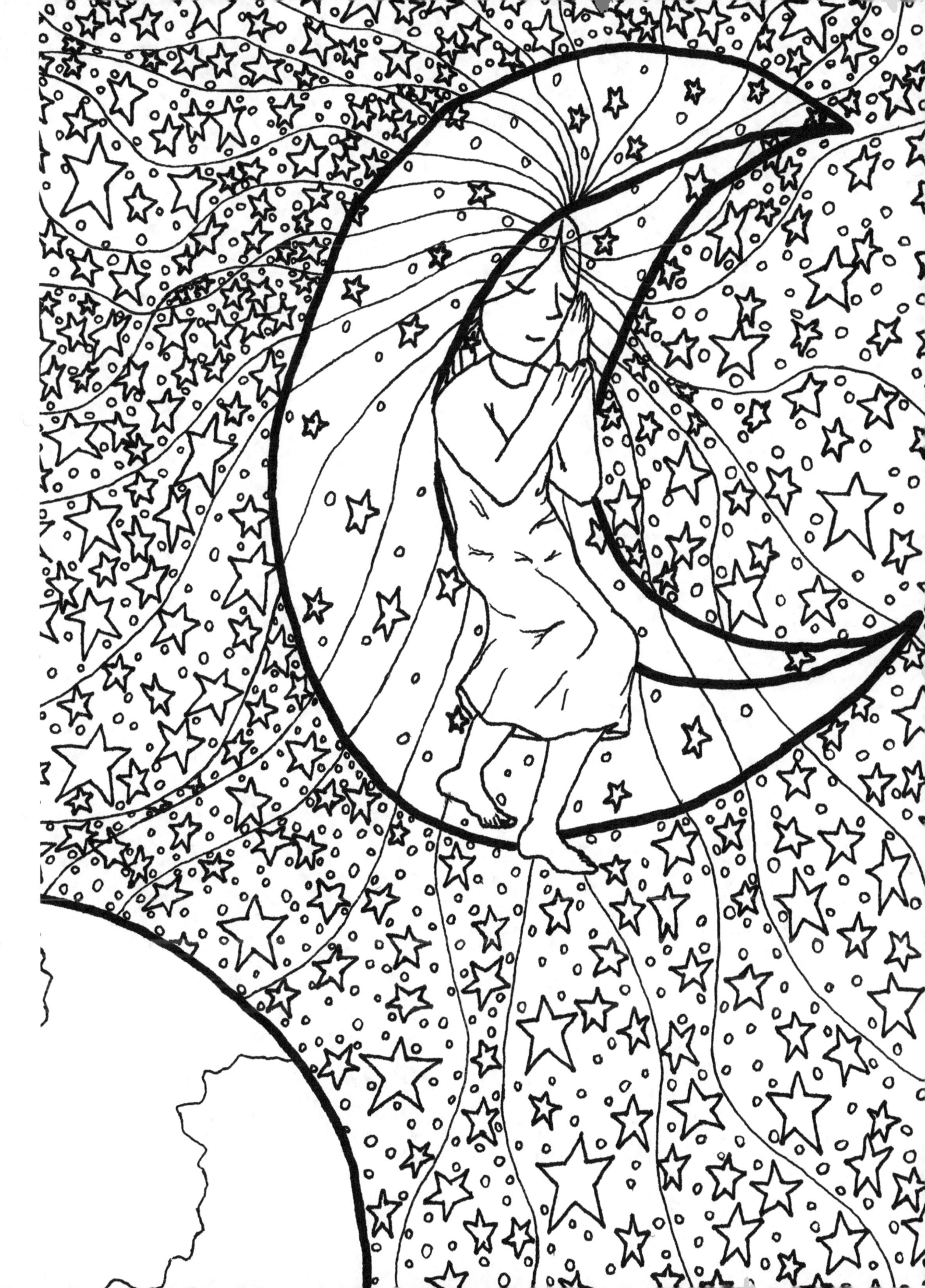

Cosmic Dreams

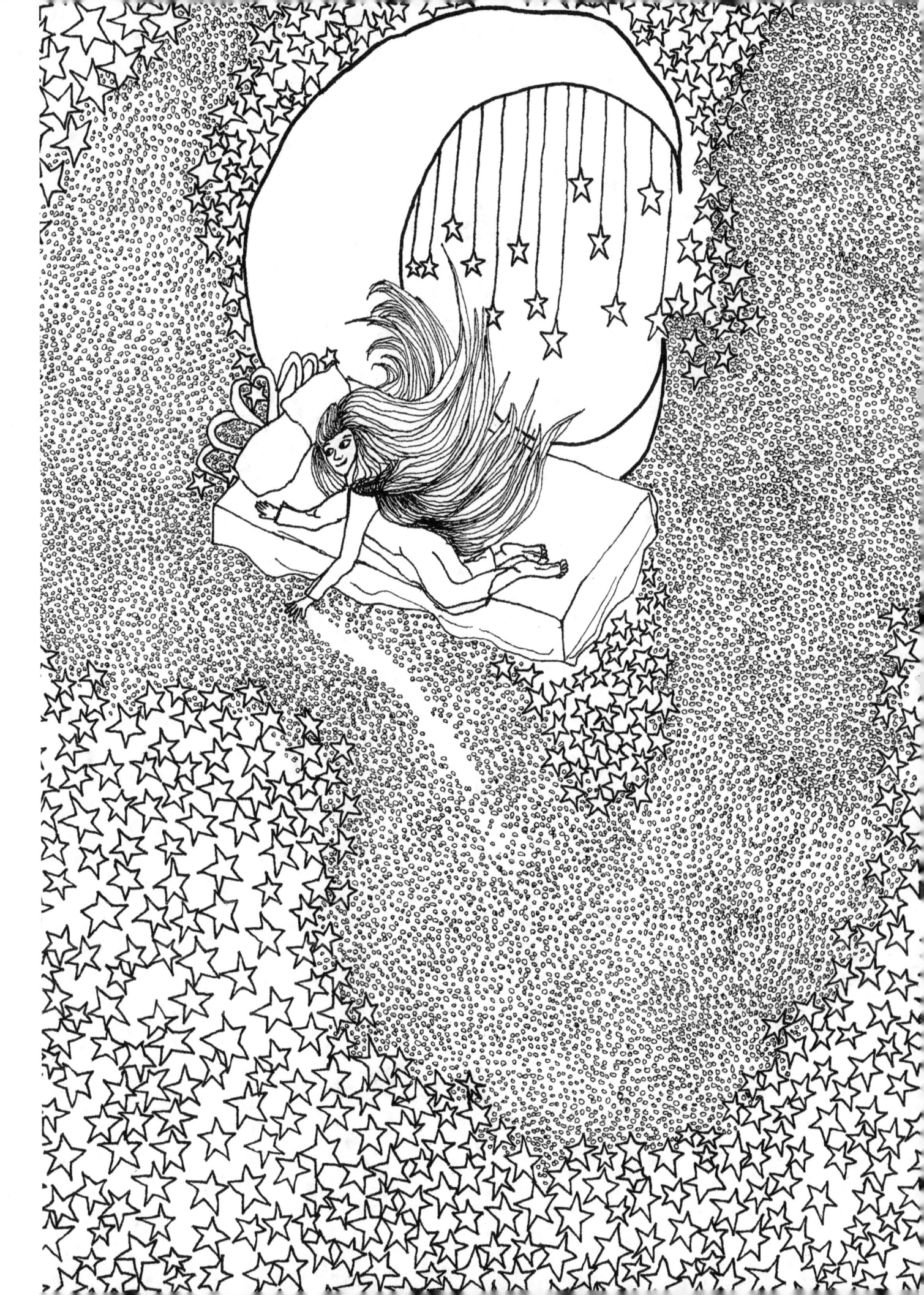

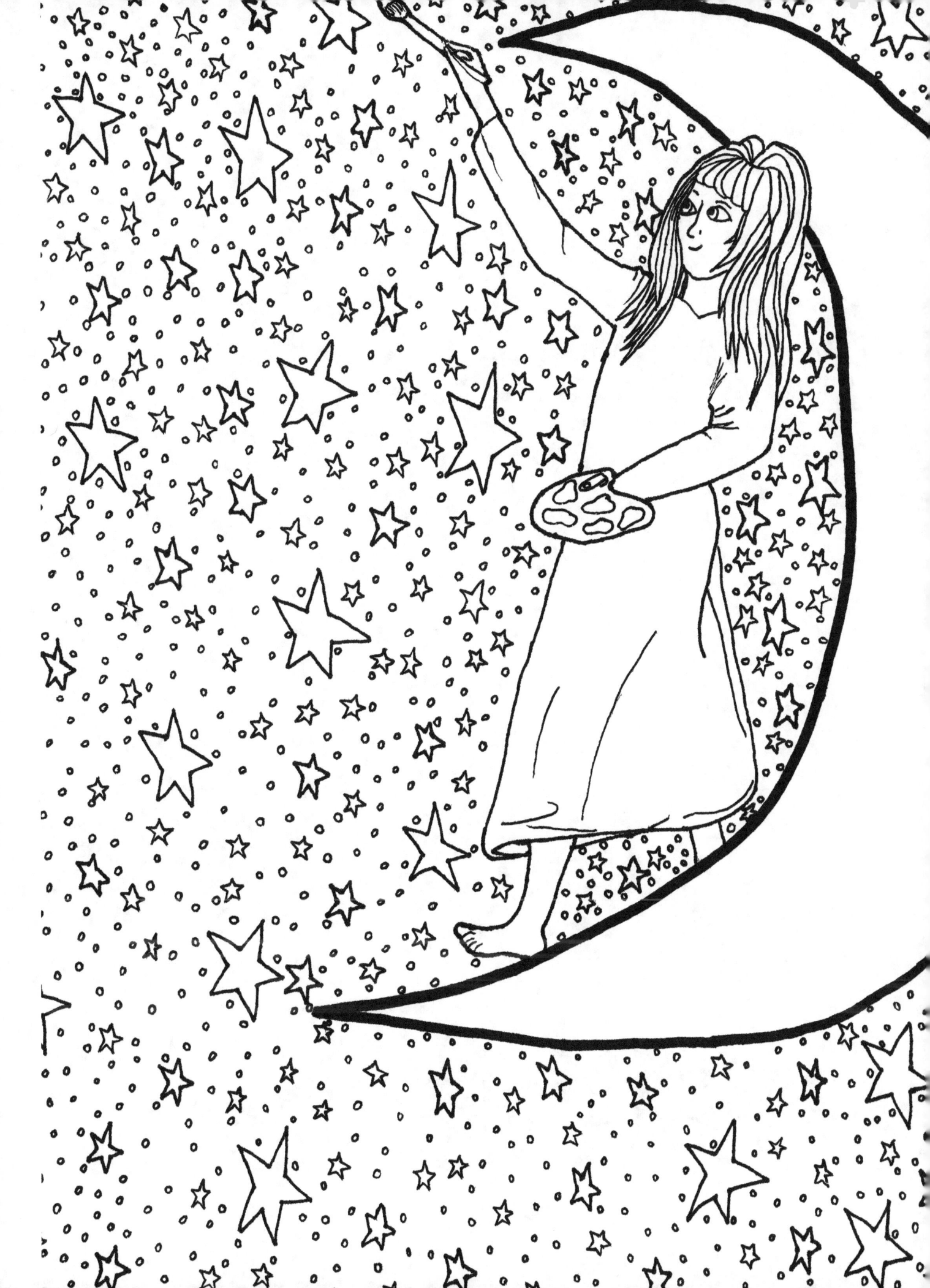

☆☆ Cosmic ☆ Dreams ☆☆

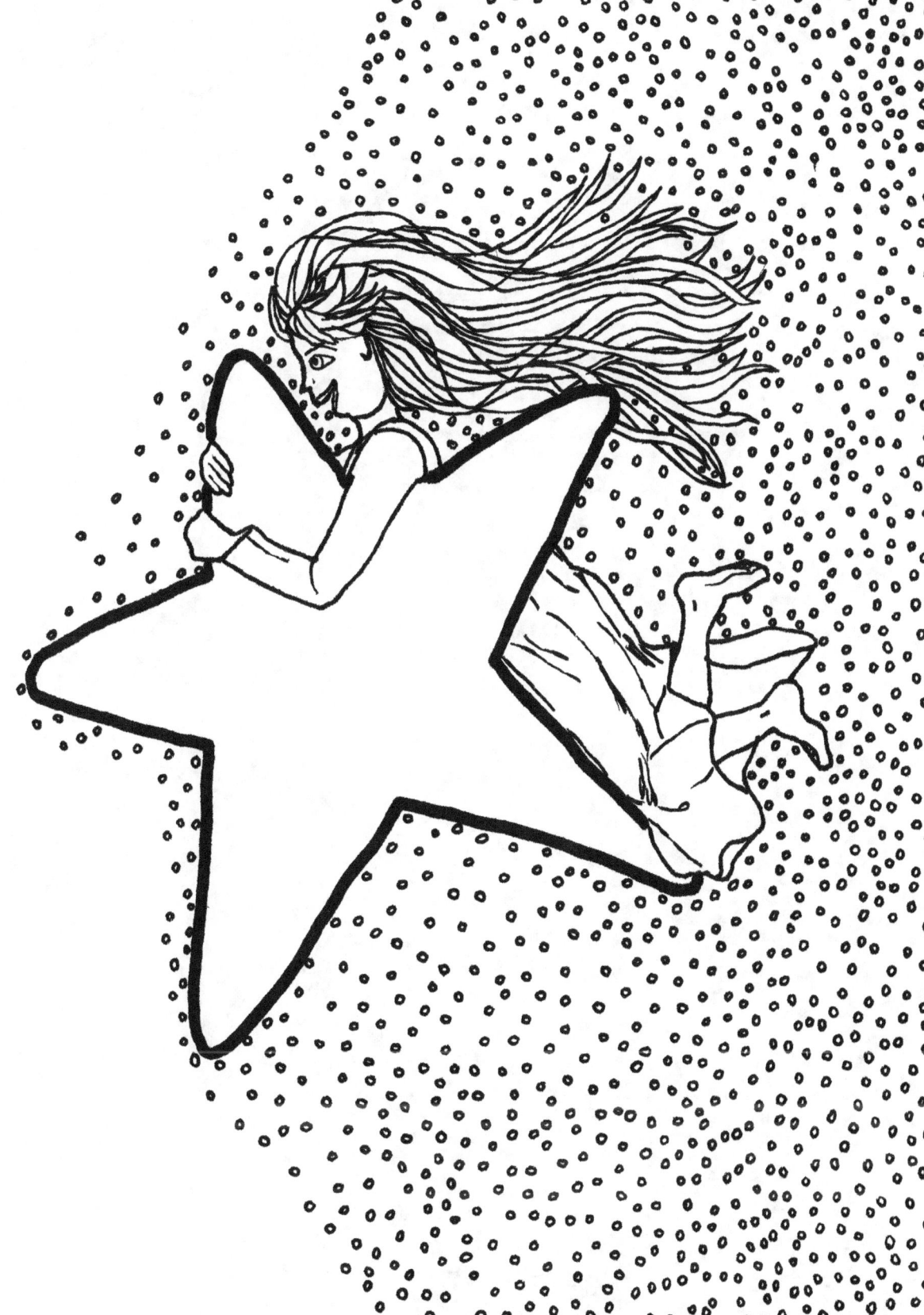

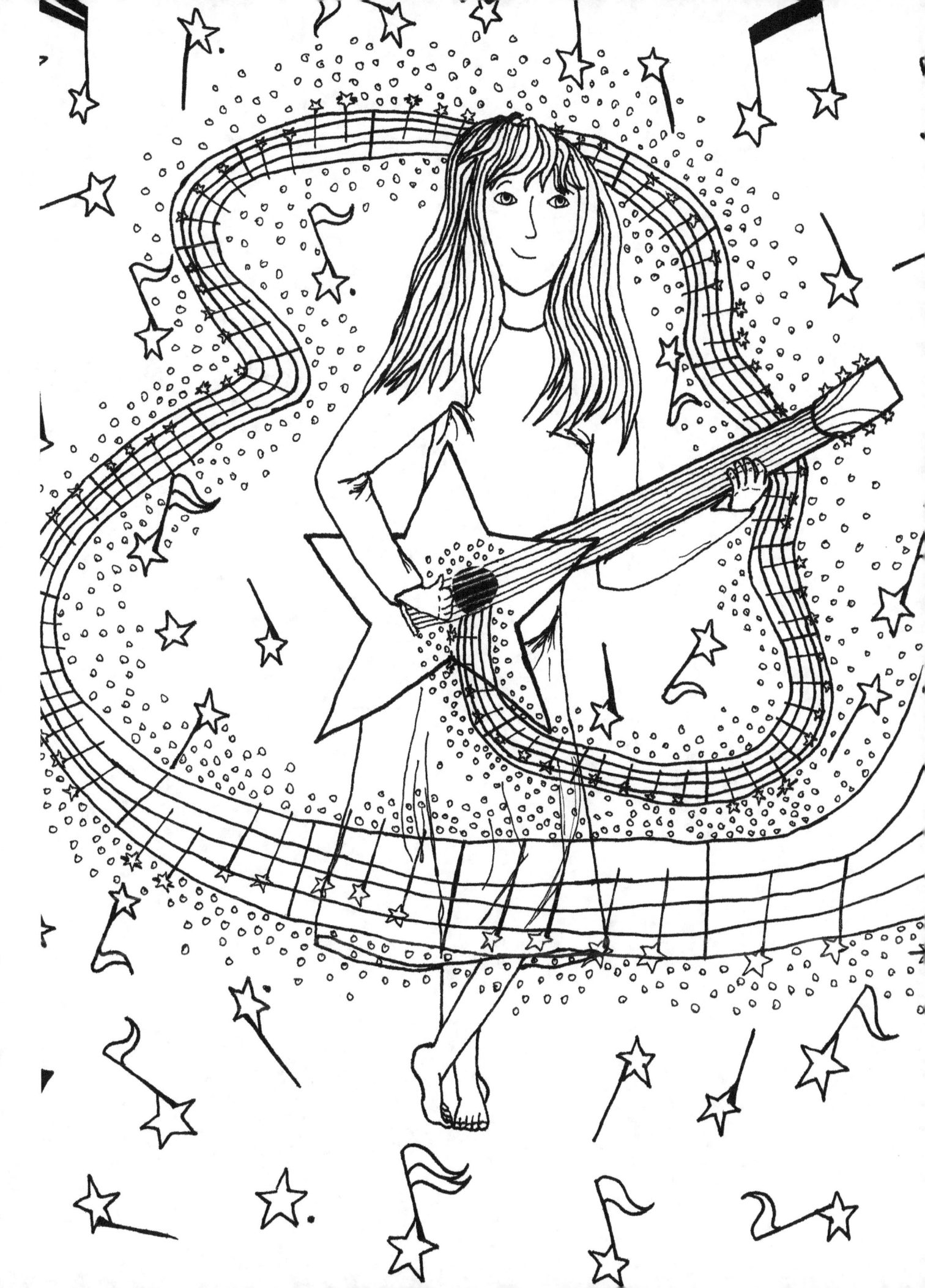

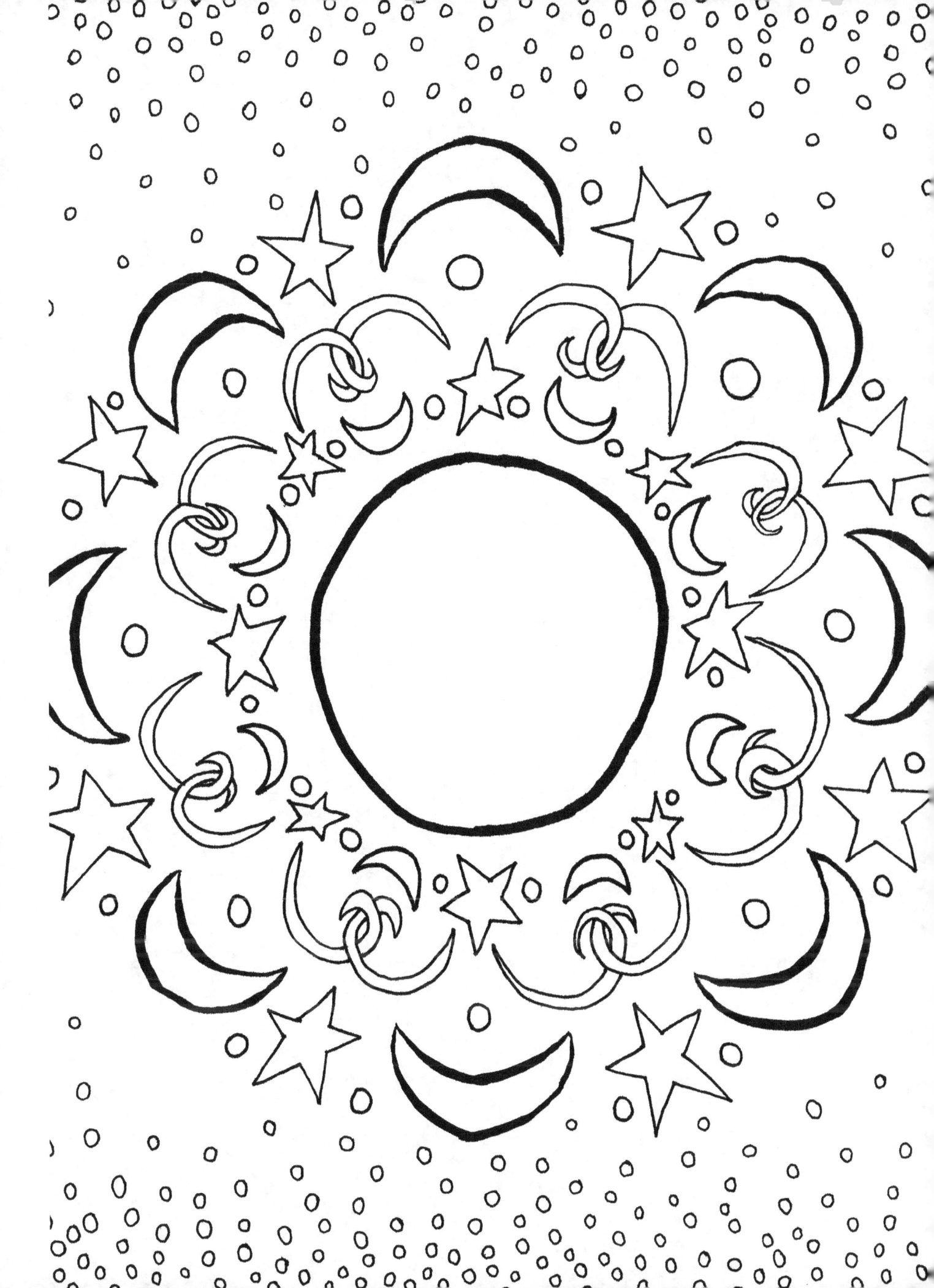

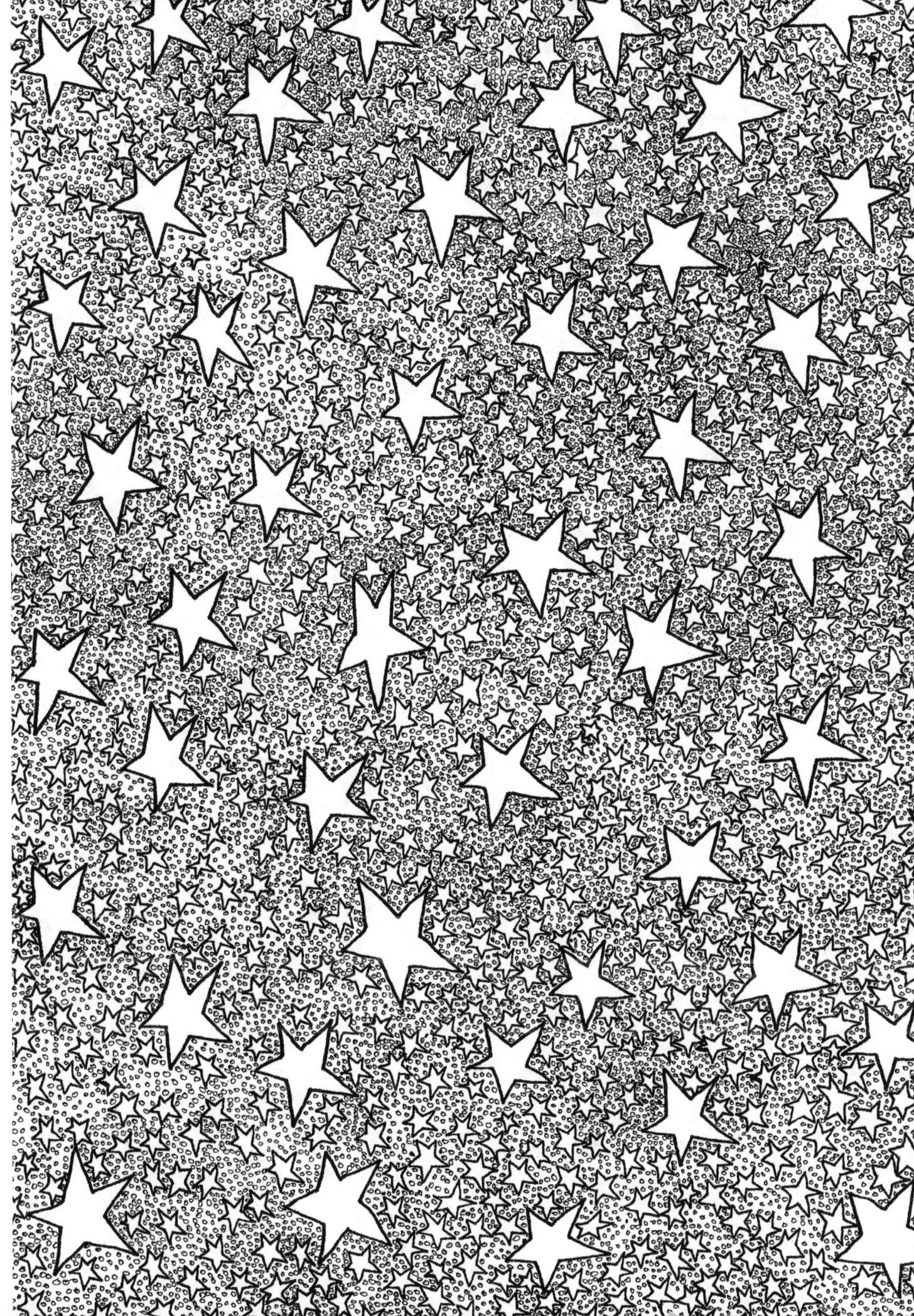

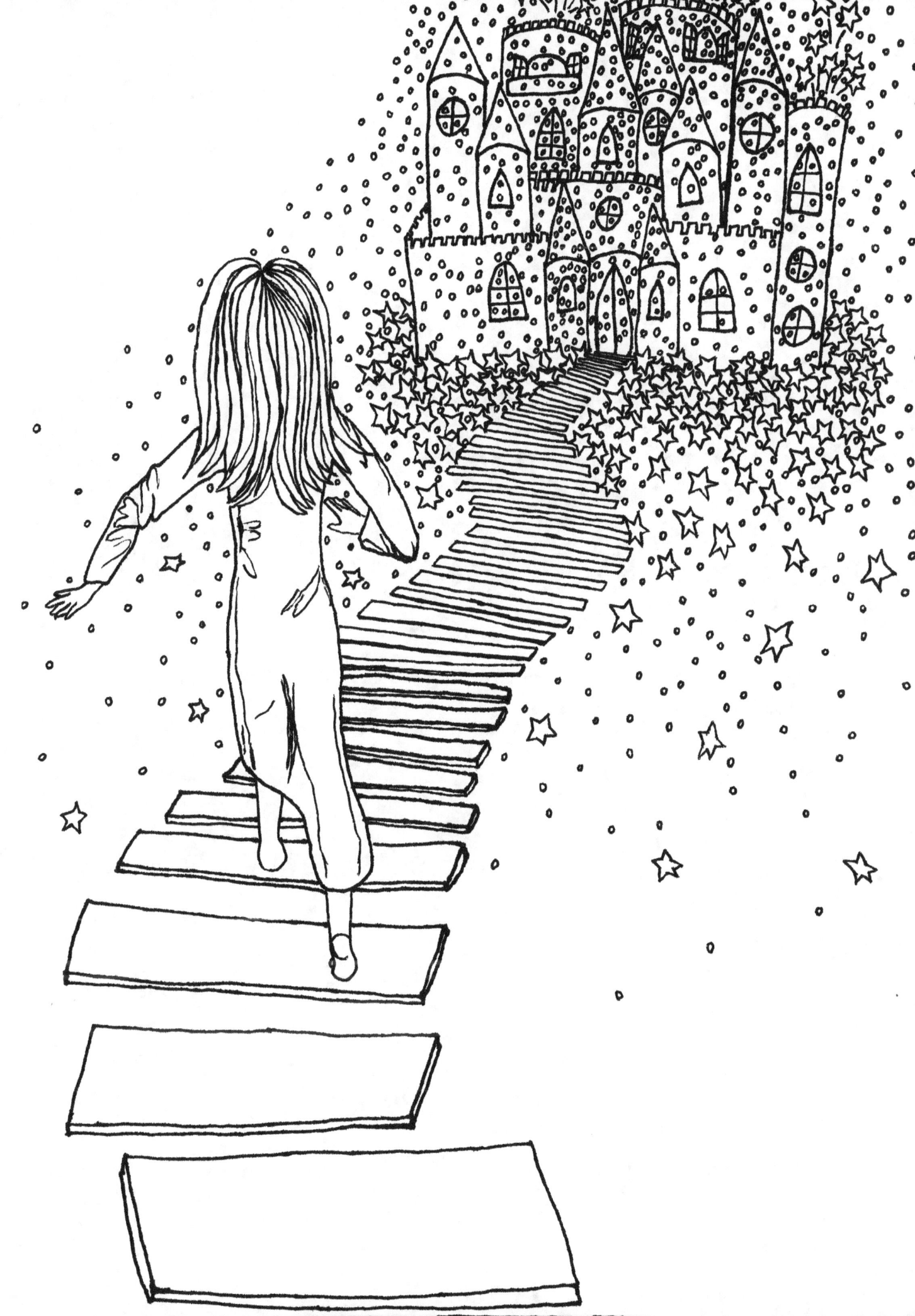

☆⭐☆ Cosmic ⭐ Dreams ⭐☆☆

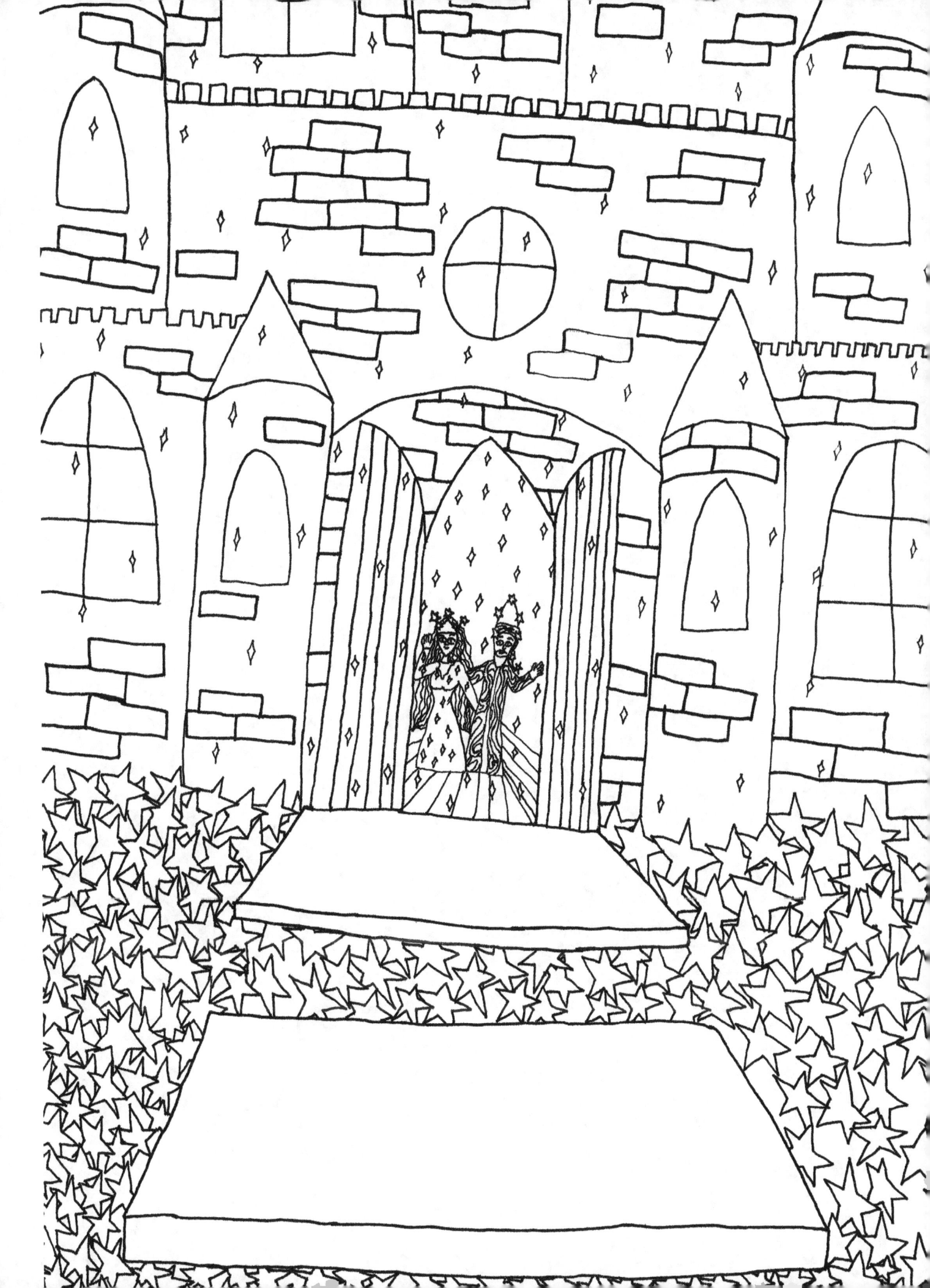

Cosmic Dreams

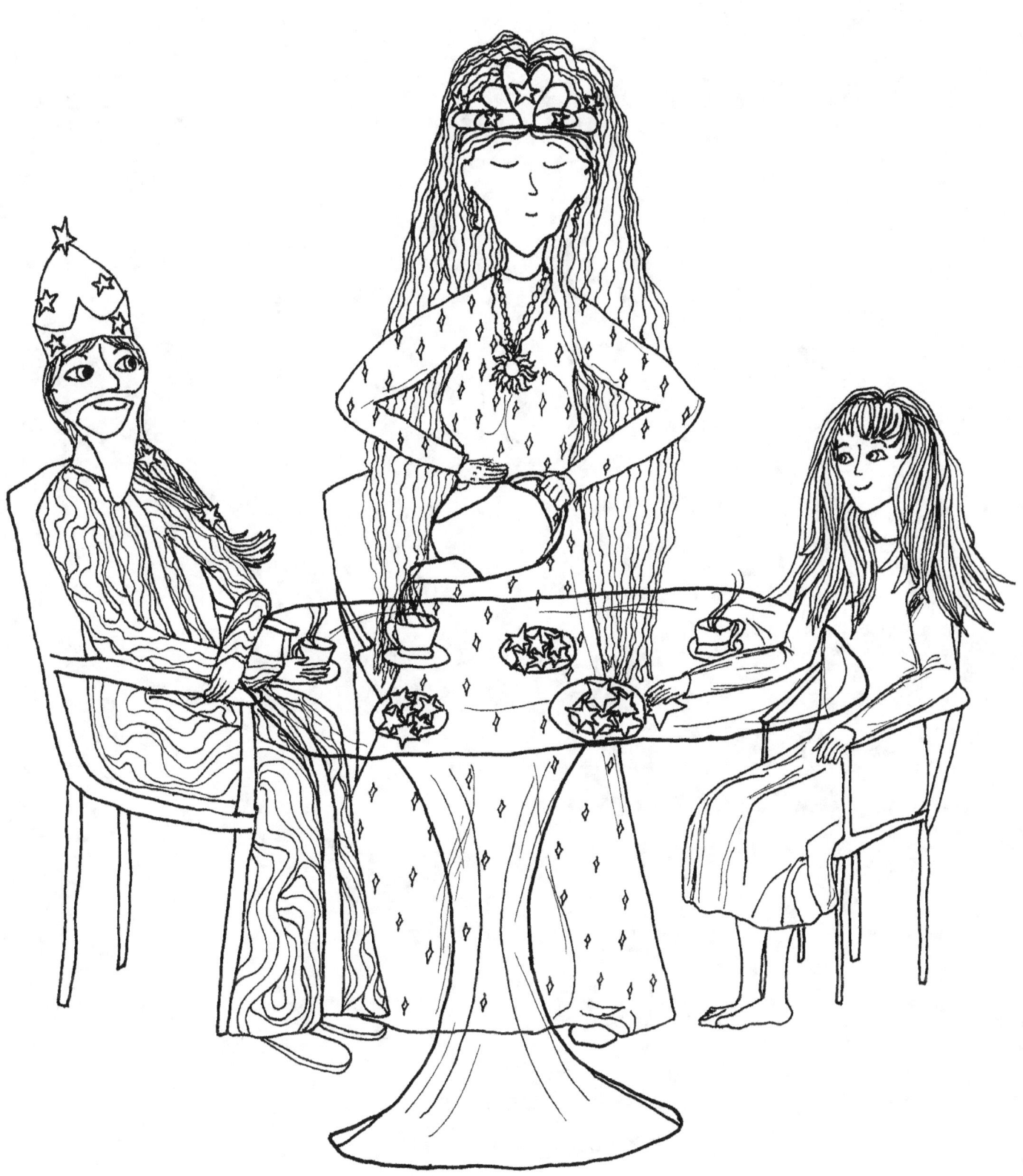

Cosmic Dreams

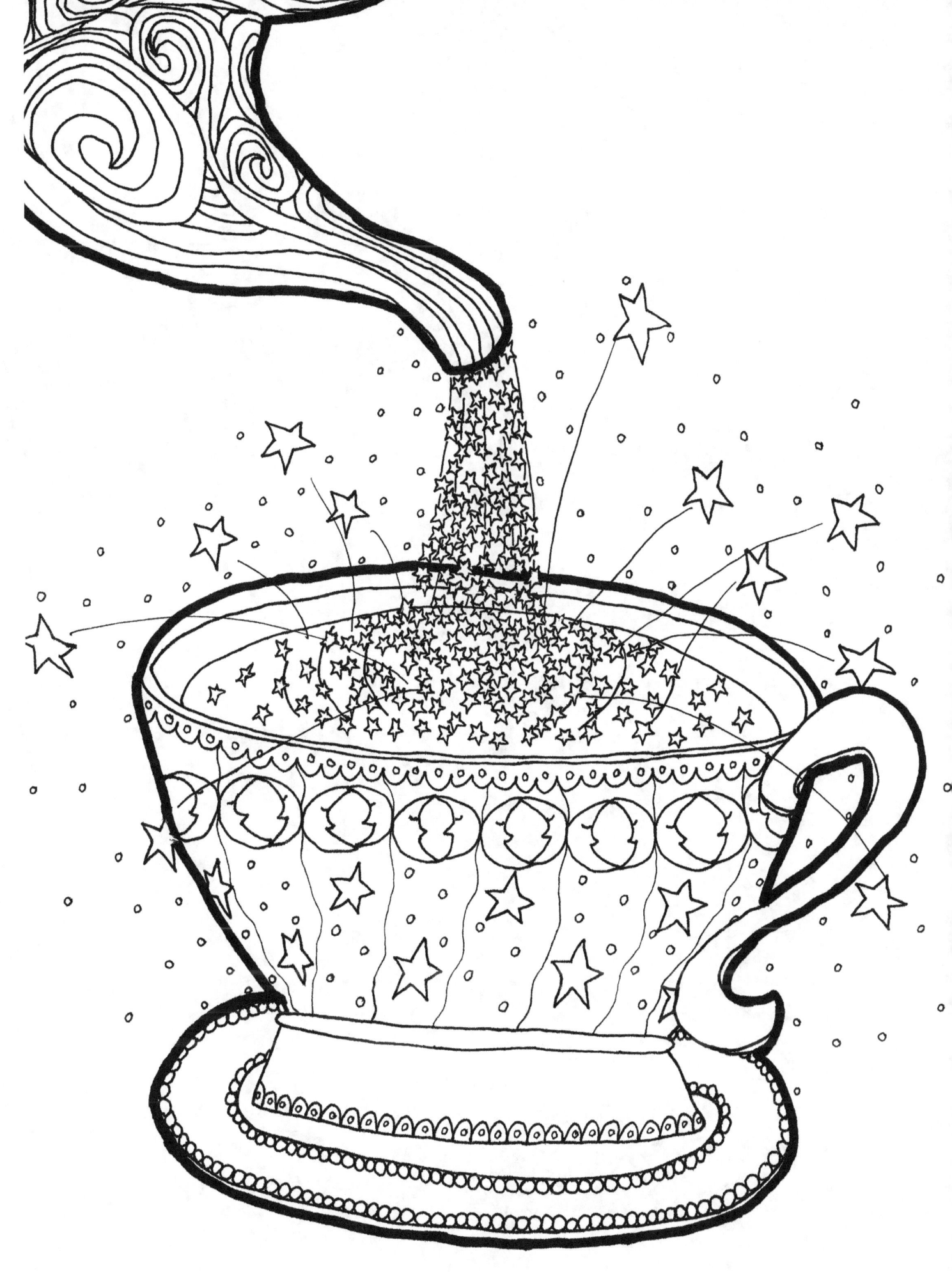

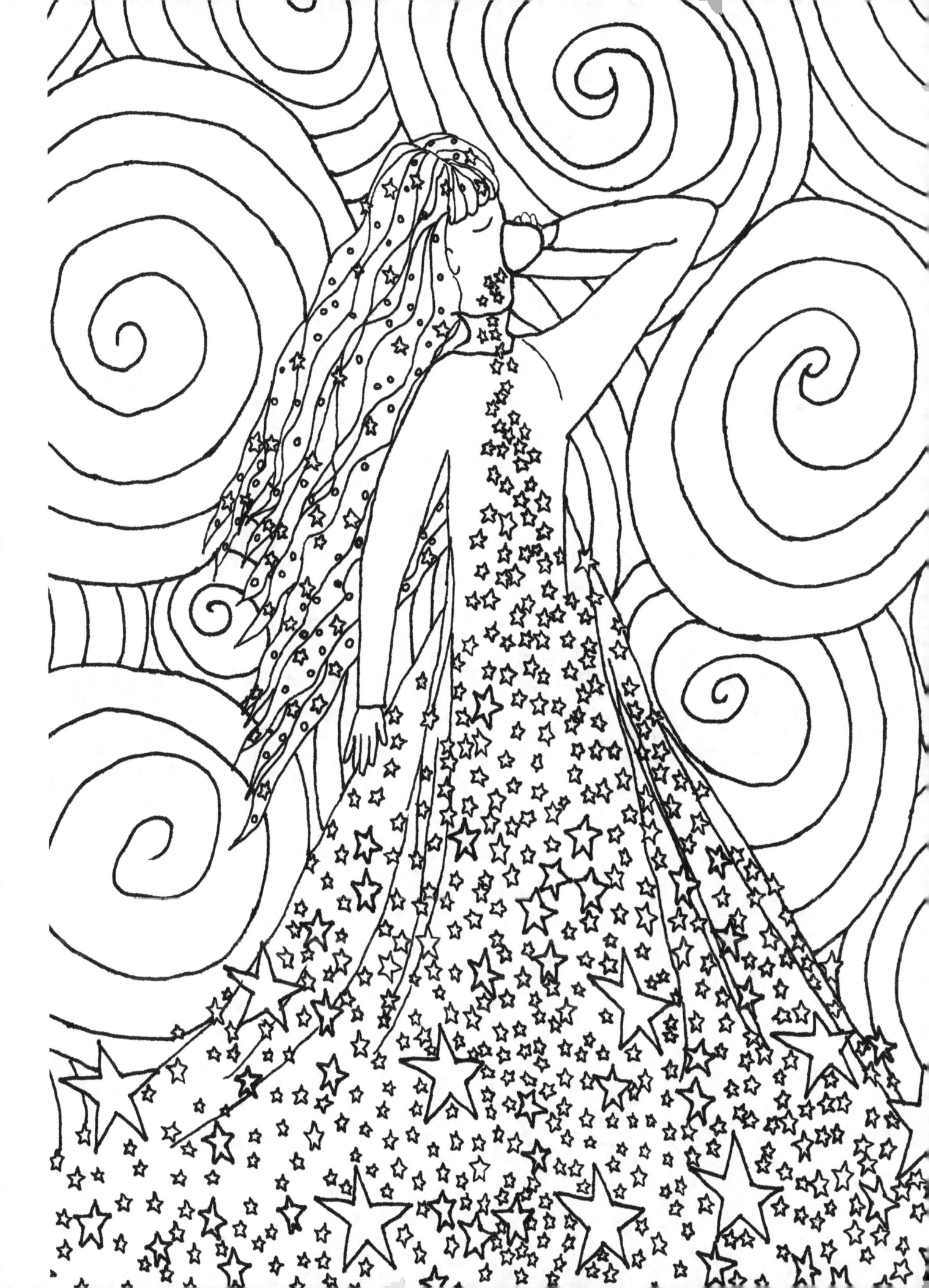

Cosmic Dreams

☆⭐☆ ☆⭐☆ ☆⭐☆

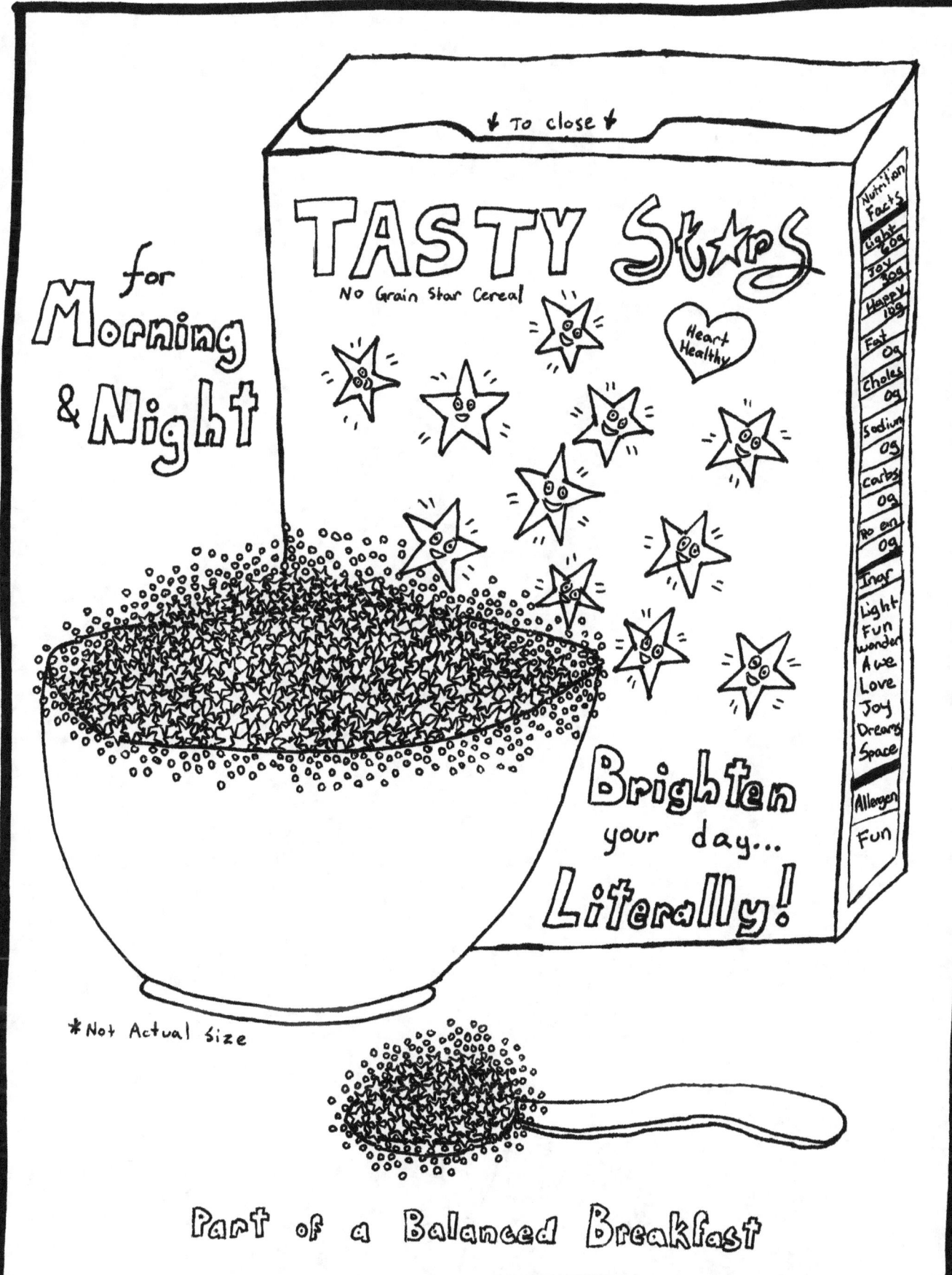

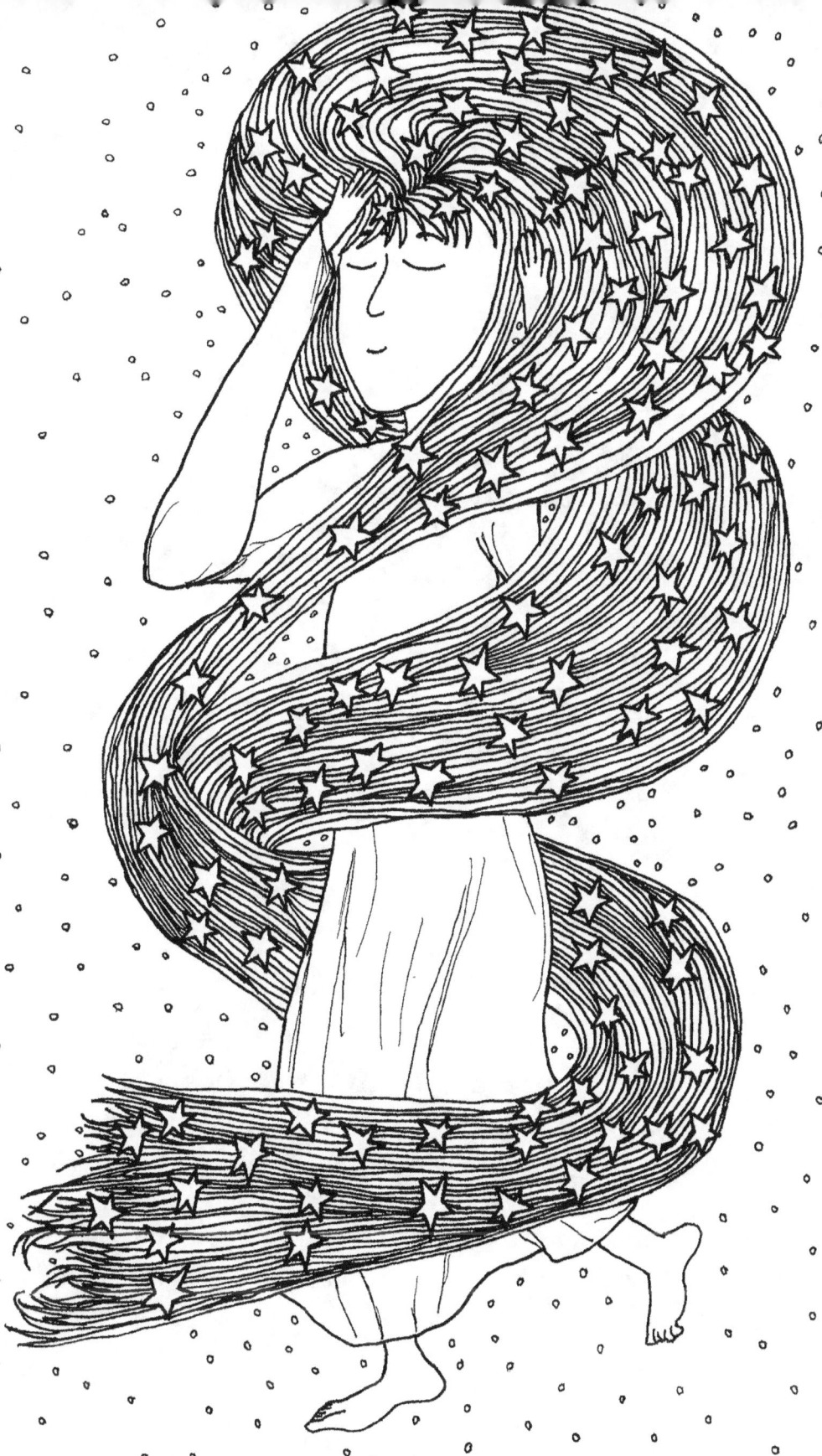

Cosmic Dreams

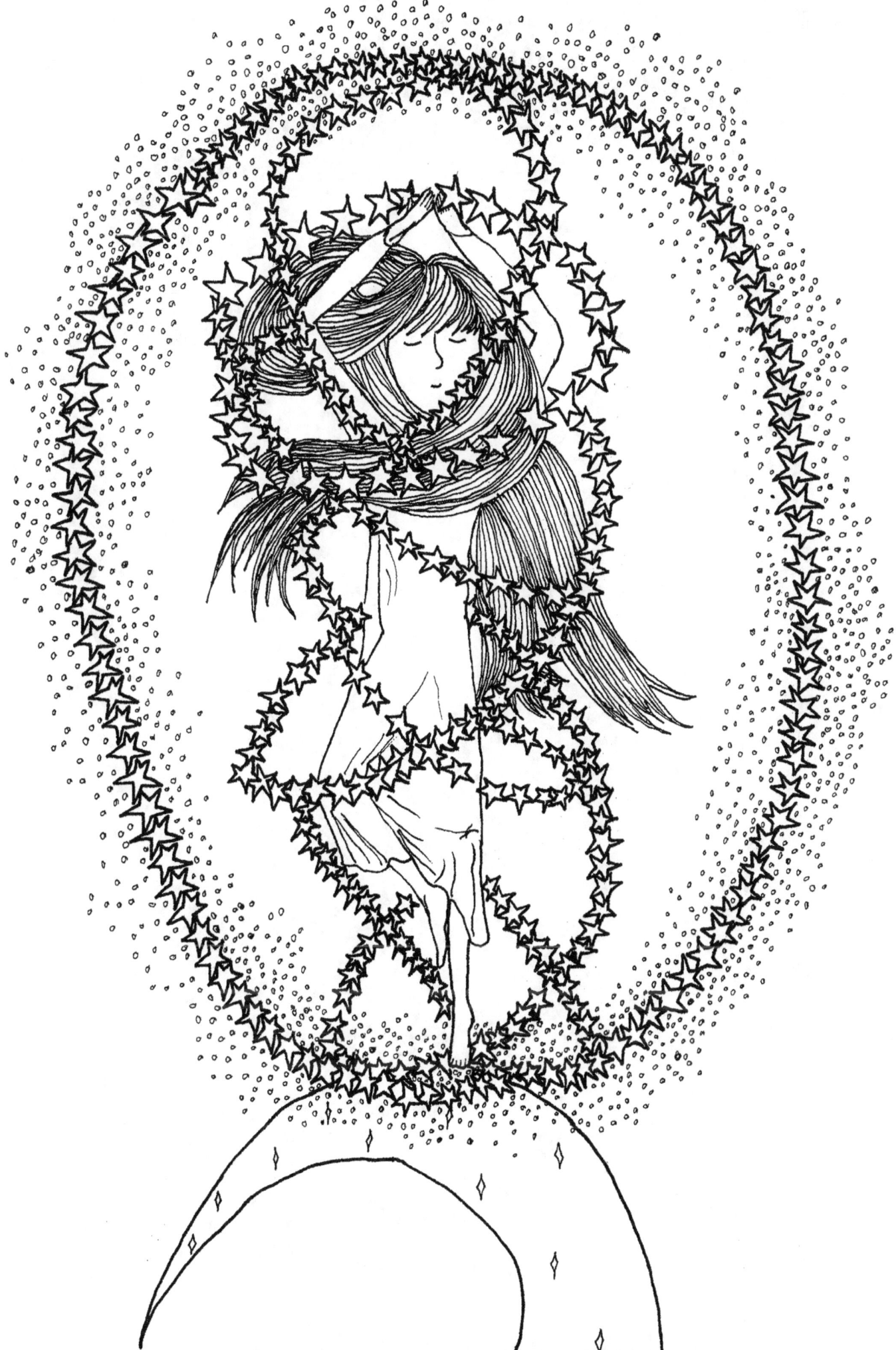

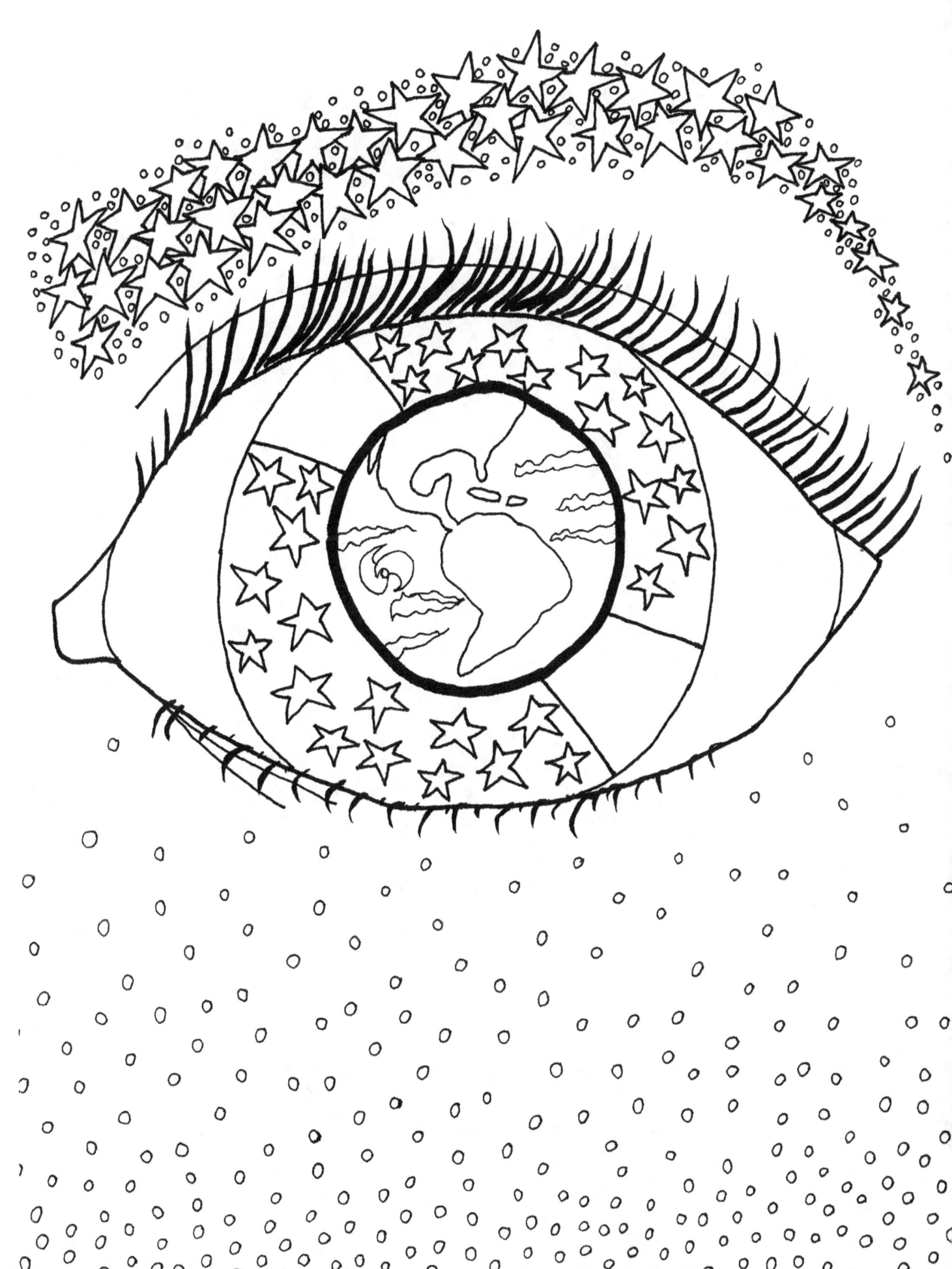

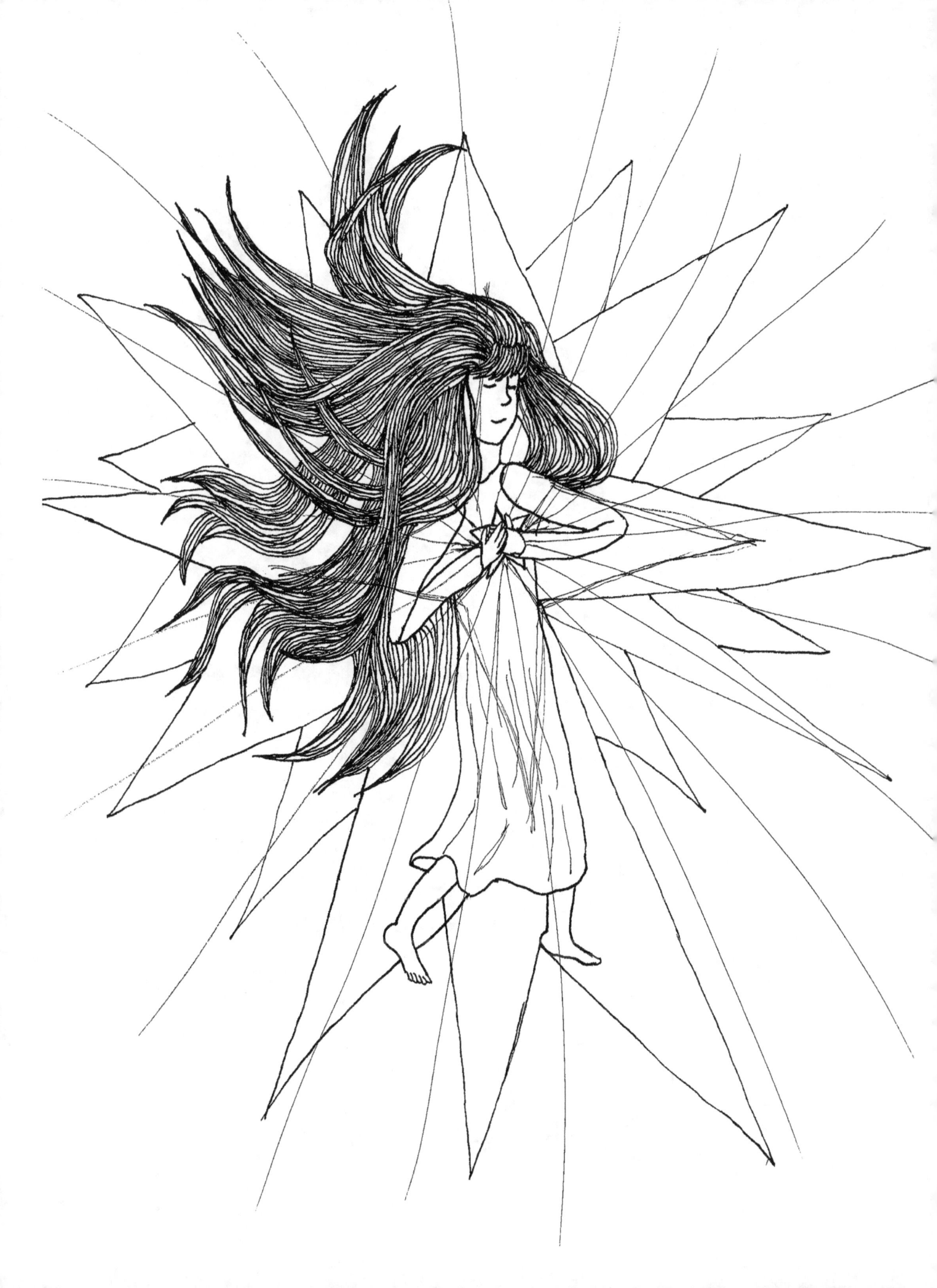

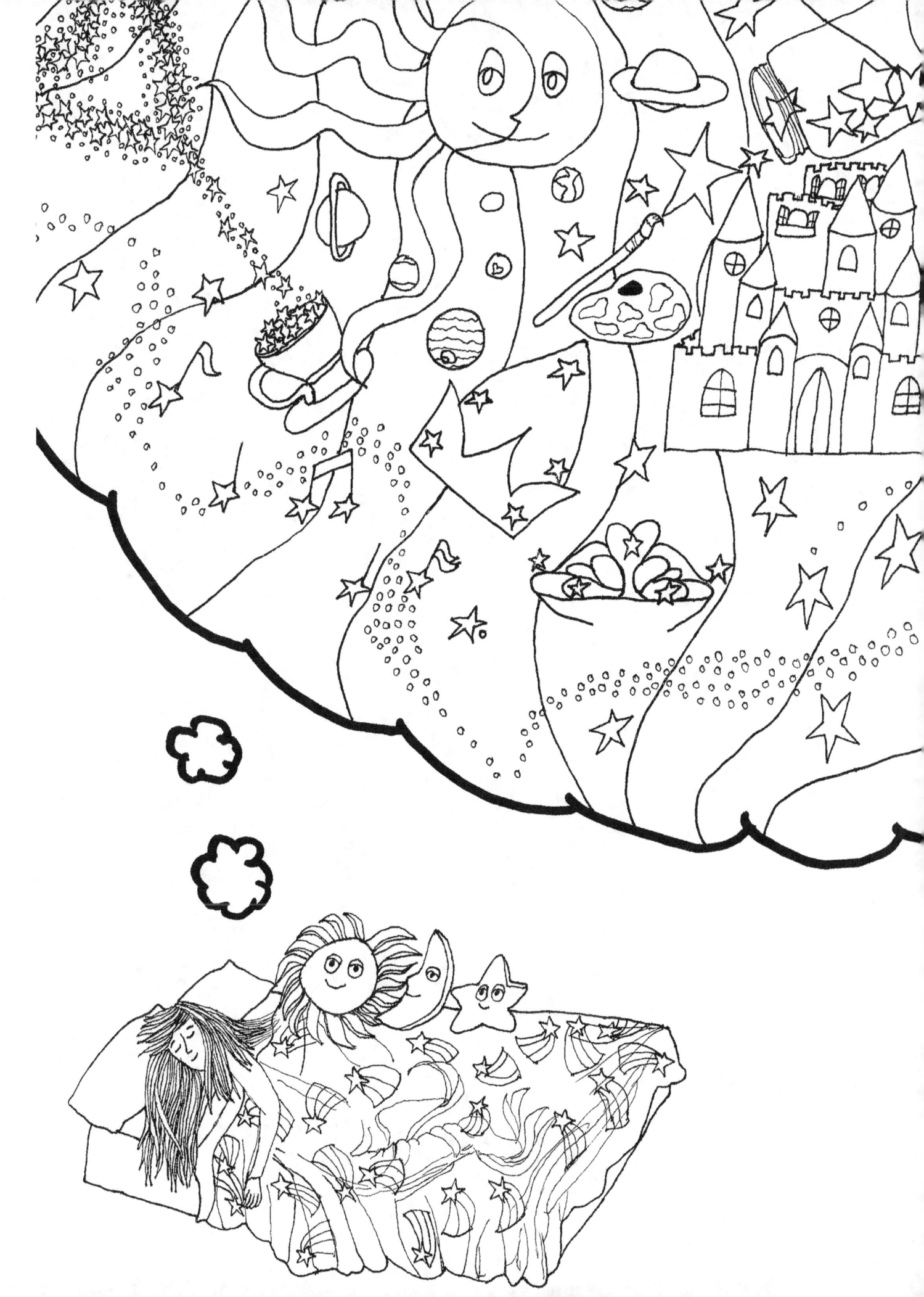

Cosmic Dreams

Color Test Page

Test your tools here!